PIANO **Listen & Learn**
HOMESPUN MUSIC INSTRUCTION

Warren
BERNHARDT
TEACHES
Jazz Piano
VOL. 1

A Hands-On Course in
Improvisation and Technique

*Featuring a Comprehensive
Audio Lesson on CD*

T0051156

Cover Photo by Happy Traum

Audio Editor: Ted Orr

Mastered by: Ted Orr at
Nevessa Productions, Woodstock, N.Y.

Produced by Happy Traum for Homespun Tapes

ISBN 0-7935-7276-2

EXCLUSIVELY DISTRIBUTED BY

HAL•LEONARD®
CORPORATION
7777 W. BLUEMOUND RD. P.O. BOX 13819 MILWAUKEE, WI 53213

© 1997 HOMESPUN TAPES LTD.
BOX 694
WOODSTOCK, NY 12498-0694
All Rights Reserved

Visit Hal Leonard Online at **www.halleonard.com**

Visit Homespun Tapes on the internet at **http://www.homespuntapes.com**

Table of Contents

CD instruction makes it easy! Find the section of the lesson you want with the press of a finger; play that segment over and over until you've mastered it; easily skip over parts you've already mastered—no clumsy rewinding or fast-forwarding to find your spot; listen with the best possible audio fidelity; follow along track-by-track with the book. This book contains music examples and all of the instructional songs from the CD, and are labeled with track icons (◆) for the ease of locating the corresponding tracks.

◆ Opening Music

◆ Introduction

Jazz piano. That's what we're here to discuss. My name is Warren Bernhardt and it's very nice to be with you. We are going to be dealing specifically with jazz improvisation on the piano.

I am assuming that you know how to read music, that you are familiar with standard chord symbols and that you know how to play all the major and minor scales.

◆ Diatonic Scales and Notation

I'd like to start with some basics and talk about notation, so that we have a clear understanding of what we're working with.

For instance, if we're playing in the key of F major and you see the notational symbol for an F major chord written, you start with a F major scale.

Beginning with the tonic, we number the tones of the scale as in the example below.

Scale tones in key of F

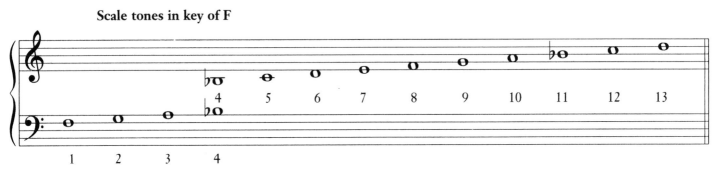

If you see an altered chord, the choice of which scale to use becomes a little more complicated. If you change one or more of the notes in the chord to a tone that's not in the diatonic scale, in your mind's eye you have to change the notes of the scale you use.

For instance, let's suppose we see an F7(♭5) chord. F7(♭5) is spelled as follows:

F7(♭5)

An F7(♭5) chord contains a lowered fifth and a minor seventh interval. Therefore, both the fifth and seventh of a major scale are changed to better suit the underlying chord [F7(♭5)].

Diatonic Scale of F7(♭5)

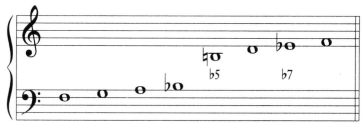

Similarly, an F7, F9 or F13 contains an interval of a flatted seventh. The appropriate scale for an F7, F9 or F13 chord is an F major scale with a lowered seventh. This scale contains the same accidentals as a B flat major scale.

Diatonic Scale of F7, F9 or F13

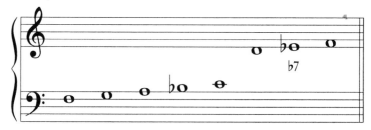

You can see that as the chord voicings change, the choice of which scale to use changes.

The reason I'm talking about chords and related scales so much is that when we build an improvisation, it's going to start with a thorough knowledge of the relationship between chords and scales.

◆ 4 II–V–I Chords

Let's work on a couple of very simple and familiar progressions that are often found in the popular song. I'll show you how scales can be used in these progressions to build an improvisation.

The II–V–I progression is very common. You've heard it a million times. (By the way, the roman numerals refer to the relationship of the root of the chord to the key.)

In the key of C major, the II chord (built on the second degree of the scale) is D minor or Dm7, the V chord is G or G7 and the I chord is some form of a C chord.

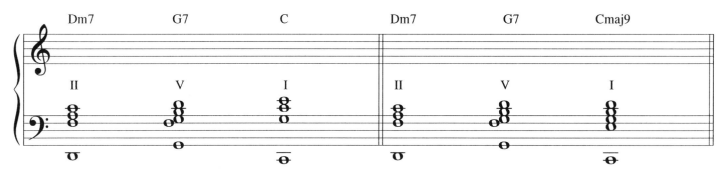

The II–V–I progression comes in several different varieties. The following example illustrates a few of the many possibilities. Note the smooth voice leading from chord to chord.

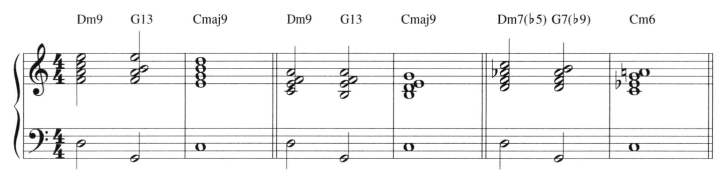

I very highly advise you to figure out the II–V–I progression in every different key.

Eventually you want to be able to play with facility in every key, so I urge you to practice these chords in various keys.

It is also helpful to practice the II–V progressions that don't ever resolve to the I chord (tonic). These types of progressions are also common in jazz. See the following example.

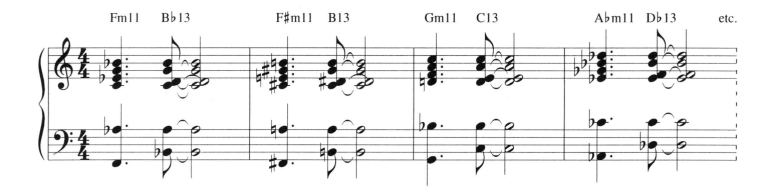

◆5 Melodic Development

Let's go back to the F major scale and talk about what we're going to do with it melodically before we get too far along in chords.

Let's say we're going to play a melody using only the notes in the F major scale, something like the following example:

In this example, I'm only using the tones of the F major scale. See how interesting a simple major scale can sound. Of course, you can also add grace notes and other embellishments that are not part of the F major scale.

Other chords in the key of F will also work with the F major scale, including the IIm chord, or Gm7, and the V chord, or C7.

So we could take the II–V–I progression in the key of F major and improvise over it, using only the tones of the F major scale.

You could also go to the D minor chord, turning the progression into a II–V–I–VI progression, which is also very common in the popular song.

Play on an F scale using chords below

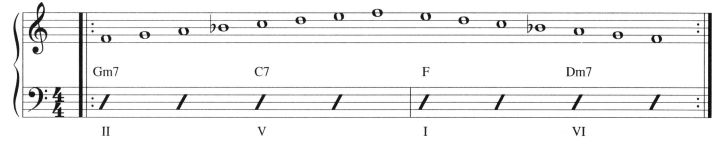

◆6 Swing Feel

When you are playing a melody in jazz, the time often has an underlying triplet feel. We call this a swing feel.

As you improvise, try to make the solo lines swing. To create a swing feel, eighth notes are played in a different fashion than in traditional forms of music. The best way to "feel" a swing eighth note is to think of an underlying triplet feel.

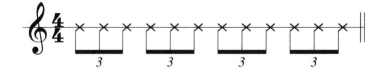

Swing eighths should be aligned with the first and third pulses of an eighth-note triplet.

Written rhythm

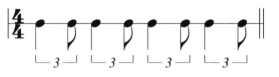

Is played as:

Written eighths

Are played as:

A good way to practice a swing feel is with a metronome. A click track or drum machine with a snare beat will also work.

Choose a tempo that's moderate, a walking tempo, and play with it. Try to get a swing feel.

You'll notice that in the recorded example I never strayed from the F major scale in the right hand.

Piano Approach

There's another aspect to playing the piano, which is hand independence. You have to think of a melody with your right hand, while playing chordal voicings with your left.

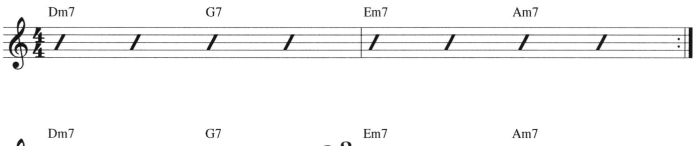

II–V–III–VI Progression in C

Let's move out of the key of F for a moment.

Here's a simple progression in C major, using the C major scale.

We call this progression the II–V–III–VI progression.

In the key of C major, the II chord is Dm7, the V chord is G7, the III chord is Em7 and the VI chord is Am7. We're playing two beats on each chord.

Below, I've written out the scale tones for each chord. Note that a C major scale will work for this progression.

(Try in other keys.)

Common Tones

When you look at the scales for the four chords in the II–V–III–VI progression as notated above, you'll notice that the scales have certain tones that are common to all. A note that is common to all scales is called a "common tone."

Miles Davis and Sonny Rollins are two example of jazz artists who would sometimes play just one common tone during an improvisation while various chords went by.

For example, in the II–V–III–VI progression, try playing just the common tone of
G.

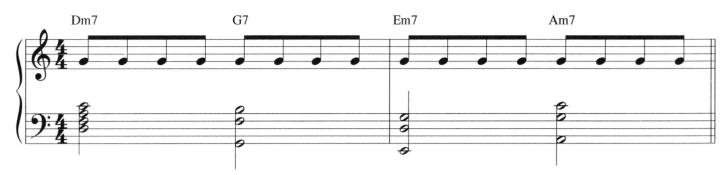

Playing the common tone of C doesn't work quite as well.

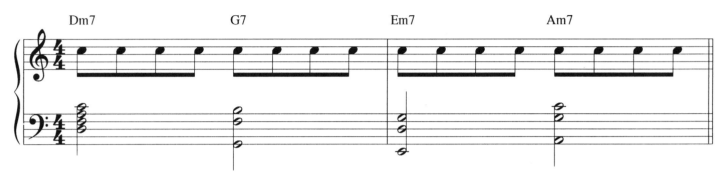

Try it with a common tone of D.

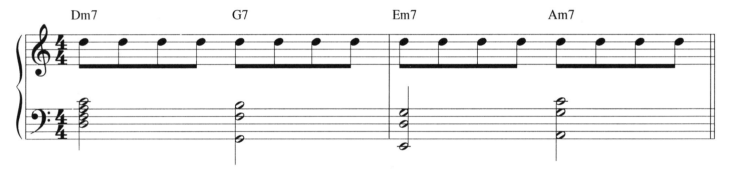

You can experiment for yourself and find common tones that you like.

🔟 Warren Plays Changes for You

On the accompanying recording, I will play the chords for you using the II–V-
–III–VI progression. Use this opportunity to play along with me. I'll play two
beats on each chord and add a walking bass line to it.

You improvise a melody. Let's try it.

⬥11 Tape Yourself

If you have a tape recorder at home you can create an accompaniment tape for yourself. Pick a simple chord progression, such as the ones we've already used. Play the chord progression in different keys. Work it out in as many keys as you can. For instance, here's the II–V–III–VI chord progression in the key of D.

Here's the same progression one half step higher in the key of E♭.

Listen to the CD for an example of a bass line and chord accompaniment in the key of C. The following example demonstrates the concept of a "walking" bass line for a II–V–III–VI progression in the key of C.

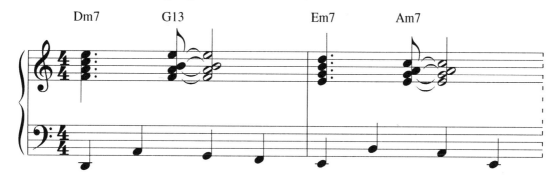

⬥12 Cm9–F13–Dm9–G13 Progression

Here's another common progression to improvise on. This progression is found in lots of tunes, including Duke Ellington's "Satin Doll."

Start with a Cm9 chord.

Then go to an F13.

Then simply move the same two chords up a whole step.

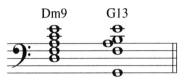

Here's the entire progression.

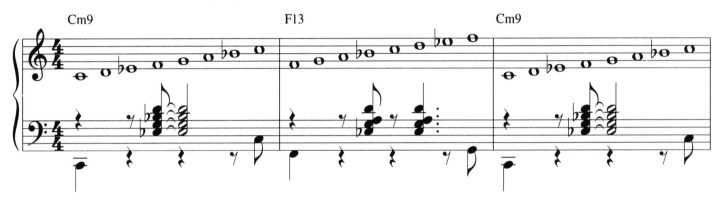

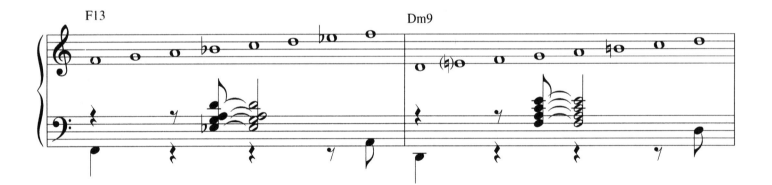

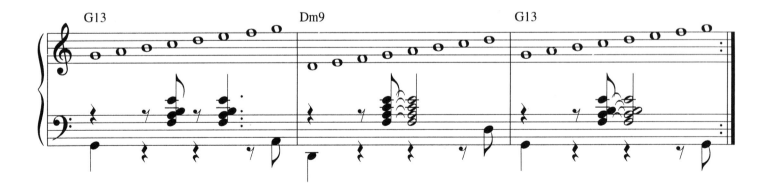

◆13 Scale Tones

In the following example, I've written out the scale tones for the right hand for the progression, because for the first time we'll be shifting scales during a progression.

Each time you get to a new chord, your thinking must shift to a new scale. You must have a firm idea of what notes you are going to play in your improvisation before you play them.

In this example, the scale tones for the Cm9 chord are going to be the C minor scale with a natural sixth and flatted seventh, which are the same notes as in the B♭ major scale.

The scale tones for the F13 chord are going to be the same notes.

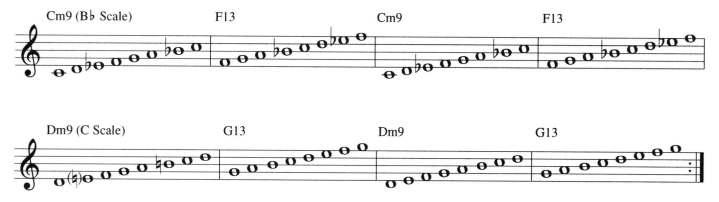

◆14 Played Example With Chords and Improvisation

In this example we will imply both a bass and harmonic function in the left hand. One of the ways this can be achieved is with smooth voice leading from the II to the V chord. In the following figure, only one note changes—the index finger moves from the seventh of the II chord to the third of the V chord.

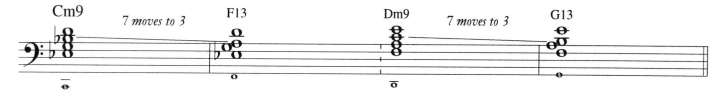

◆15 Played Example with Bass Added

Pick out notes you like to go with the following.

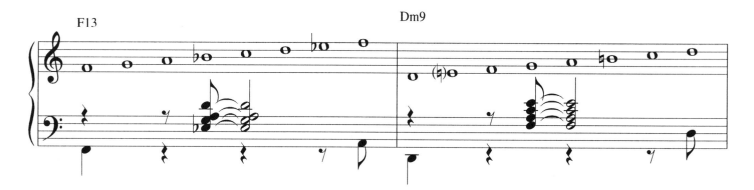

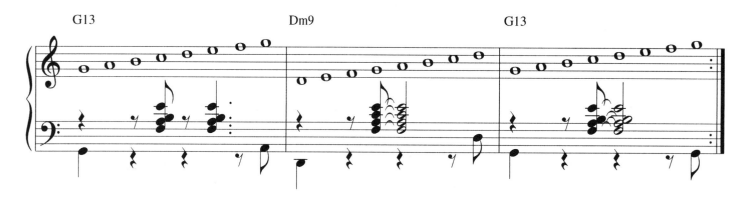

You have to try and divide your thinking into two parts, one part for each hand.

Try to get the left hand going by itself. You don't necessarily have to play the bass notes down an octave. If the jump from the root to the chord seems awkward, try moving the root up an octave.

Perhaps use a slower tempo than I use on the recording. Start slowly and get the flow going. You can pick up speed later.

◆16 Warren Plays Changes for You

I'll play the same chord progression for you. With your right hand, play an improvised melody to go with the progression while I play the left hand part.

⑰ Changing Rhythmic Feels

You'll notice that I changed the time in that example from a "two-feel" to a "four-feel."

Often, when playing jazz, you'll play the "head" of the tune with a two-feel and then play a four-feel for the improvisations over the chorus.

The feel usually comes from the bass pattern (along with the drums).

In a "four-feel," the bass usually "walks" in a steady quarter-note pulse. In a "two-feel," the bass plays two half-note pulses per bar.

Ray Brown is a great example of a bass player changing up the feel by altering the bass line.

⑱ Working in Different Keys

As an example, work on the following exercise, which is written one-half step higher than the previous example.

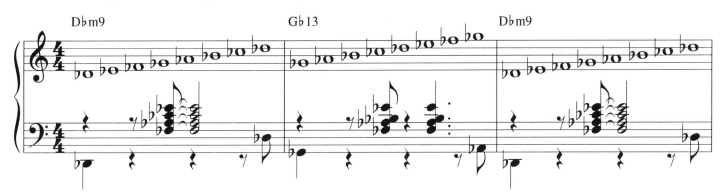

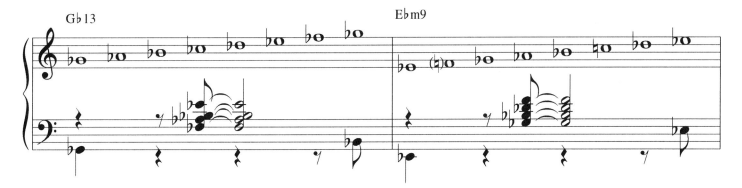

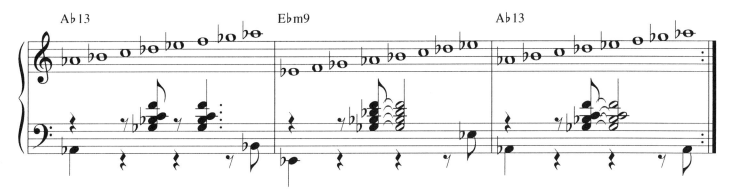

This is to get a feel for different keys on the keyboard.

Try it again, up a whole step.

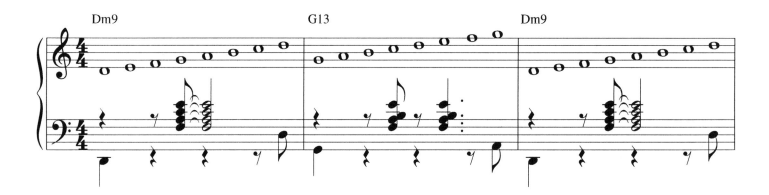

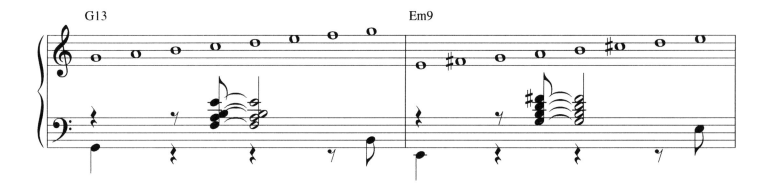

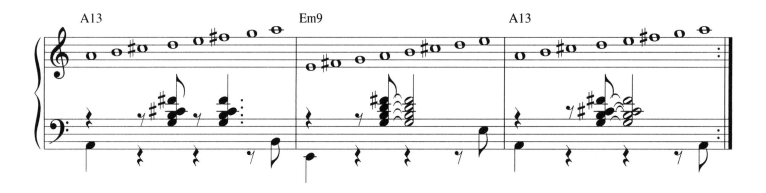

Try it in several different keys. Try all the exercises in this book in different keys in order to develop your facility for different keys and scales. Work out all the earlier examples in different keys before you proceed to the next section.

⓳ Using the Tritone

Before we get into the blues, I'd like to talk about the tritone.

The blues is a very integral part of jazz. When playing the blues, you play a lot of seventh chords. Dominant seventh chords contain the interval of a tritone.

A tritone is the interval of three whole steps either up or down.

For instance, starting on F the interval of a tritone up is to B♮. The interval of a tritone down is also to B♮.

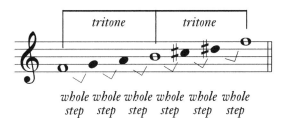

The tritone divides the octave literally in half: F to B is a tritone and B to F is a tritone.

Tritone intervals are very handy when voicing blues chords.

The dominant seventh chord is the basic type of chord common to most blues progressions. Dominant seventh chords contain an interval of a tritone, the interval from the third of the chord to the seventh..

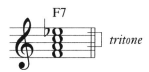

If I play a B7 (B, A, D♯) and then an E7 (E, G♯, D), you'll notice that the tritone in each chord moves down one-half step.

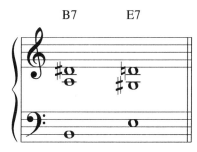

Play the following example and note that a circle of fifths progression of dominant seventh chords can be played by half-step movement of the tritone.

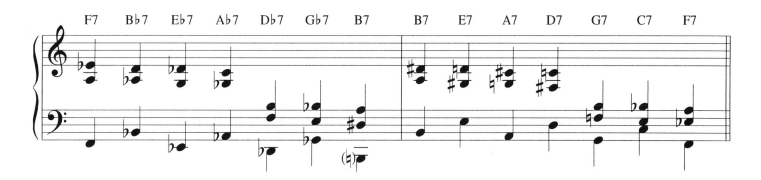

Incidentally, the *circle of fifths* progression is found in many standard jazz tunes. The most common root movement is down by a perfect fifth (or up by a perfect fourth). This progression of chords is called a *circle* because the progression will eventually cycle through all possible roots.

◆20 Using the Tritone in Blues

When we're playing the blues and using a lot of seventh chords, you can use tritone forms in the left hand, moving by one-half step to cover the basic harmony. Leave out the root of the chord, to be played either by the bass, or simply suggested by the tritone harmony.

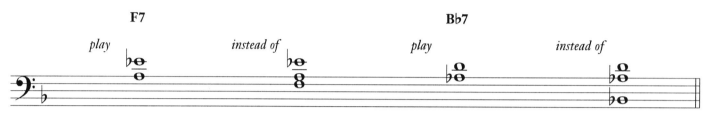

The following twelve-bar blues illustrates how easy it is to play a blues progression using tritones (third and seventh).

12 bar blues in F using tritones in left hand

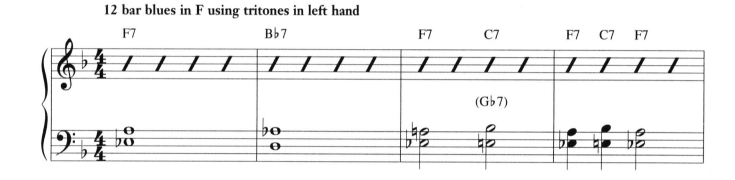

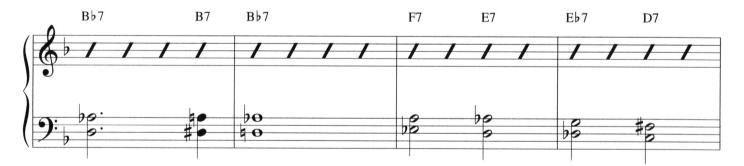

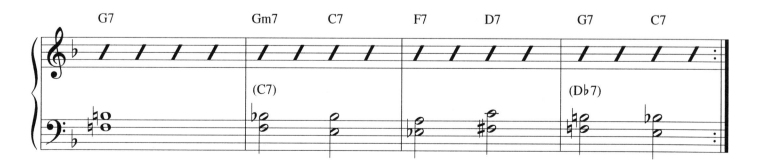

Here is an example is a typical blues lick using tritone harmony in the left hand.

◆21 The Blues Scale

What do we mean by the blues scale?

Basically, if we're playing in the key of F, we start with the tonic, or F.

In the blues, we use both the major and minor third.

The blues third is peculiar. On guitar you can bend notes and bend between the major and minor third. We can't bend notes on the piano, so we play both the major and minor thirds to create the "blue note" effect.

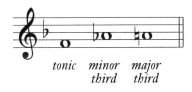

We use the fourth in the blues scale. And we use both the flatted and natural fifth, another example of "blue notes."

Thus, so far our blues scale in F consists of F, A♭, A, C♭ (or B♮) and C. Of course, we also use the flatted seventh (E♭) frequently in blues. We can also use the raised seventh (E♮) to slide into the tonic.

One can use both the second and the natural sixth, and perhaps the raised fifth degree to slide into the sixth.

Thus, the only tone we don't usually use in the blues scale is the minor second, one-half step above the tonic.

F blues scale (learn in all keys)

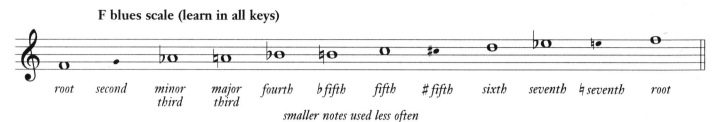

| root | second | minor third | major third | fourth | ♭ fifth | fifth | ♯ fifth | sixth | seventh | ♮ seventh | root |

smaller notes used less often

The following phrase is typical of the types of motives used over an F7 chord. Notice the variety of tones used in this example. Also note how both a minor and major third are used. Horn players and singers have the ability to play or sing the blues third (a pitch somewhere between a major and minor third). Although it is not possible to "bend" notes on the piano, both the minor and major third are often used to create the illusion of blues notes.

If you're really interested in playing the blues, you should check out Dr. John's series of Homespun video and audio tapes. Dr. John is a master of the blues and of other New Orleans piano styles, and his Homespun tapes are very instructive.

㉒ Using the Blues Scale

Listen to the recorded example of how to use the F blues scale when playing blues in F.

Experiment with the F blues scale.

Some players like to use common tones on top of a blues motive. The following figure is a typical example of this type of passage.

Once you've got the F blues scale down, practice the blues scale in other keys. Go through all the keys if possible.

23 ▸ Combining the Tritone With Scales
(Played Examples)

Listen to the recorded example of the 12-bar blues progression in F using only tritones in the left hand.

12 bar blues in F using tritones in left hand

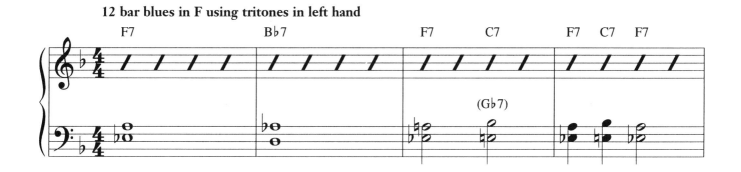

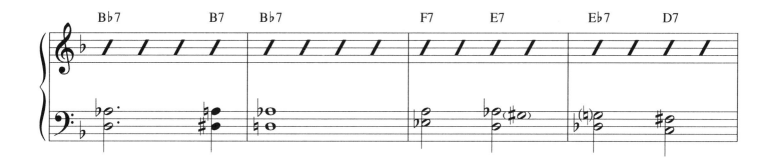

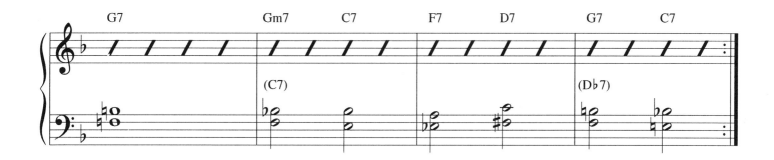

◆24 Blues Variations

This is how the left hand would be written when you add the bass note roots to the tritones. You need large hands to reach the tenths in this example

12 bar blues in F using full chords in left hand

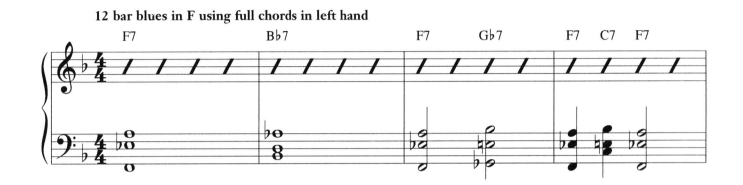

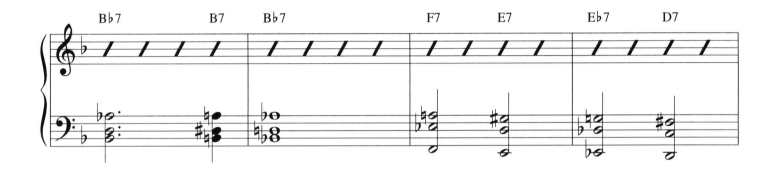

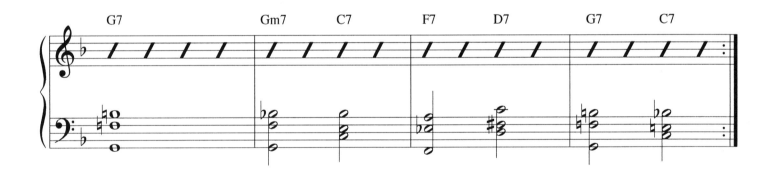

It's fun to play the blues.

The following is a modern variation of the traditional 12-bar blues. Let's call it the "new blues."

"New" blues changes

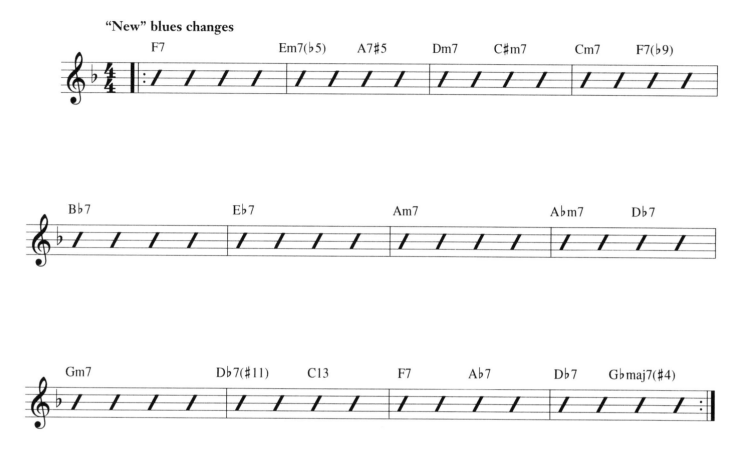

25 Warren's Blues
(16 Bar)

Here's an original bluesy exercise in A, just the basic chord changes. This is a 16-bar approach to the blues.

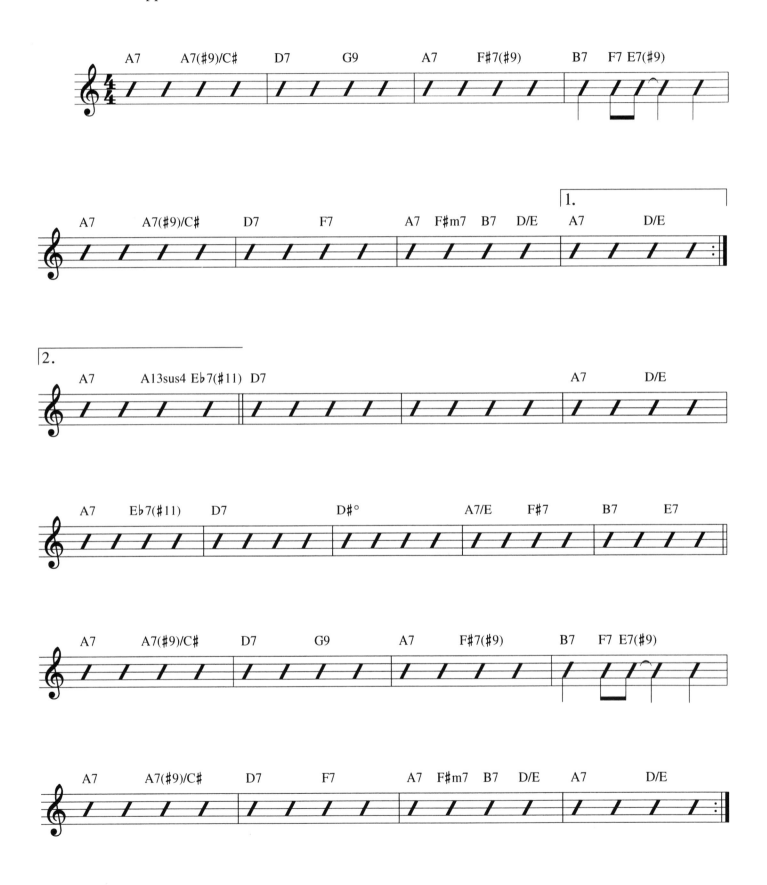

◆26 Minor Blues

The minor blues is also used often in jazz. It's a pattern similar to the standard 12-bar blues, but you play in a minor key and deal almost exclusively with minor chords. For example, playing in F minor, you begin with an F minor chord, which goes to the IV chord or B♭ minor and then back to the I, or F minor, chord.

"Minor" blues progression

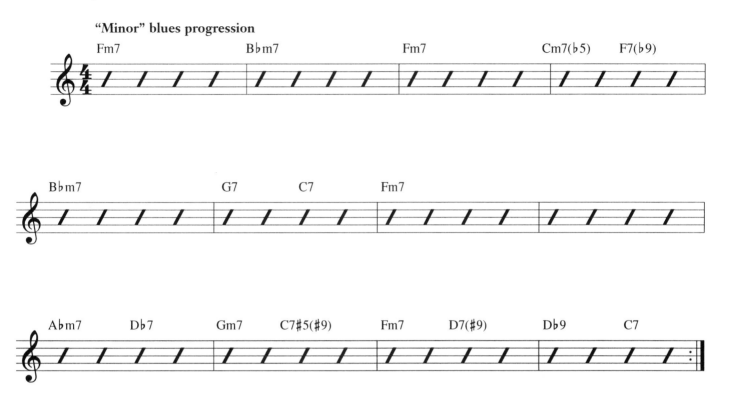

In bar 4, I use two passing chords to get back to the IV chord—Cm7(♭5) and F7(♭9).

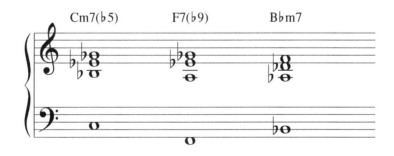

Listen to the minor blues.

You'll notice that the minor blues has a whole different mood and feel to it, as contrasted with the standard 12-bar blues.

27 "Rhythm" Changes

The following exercise is an example of what we call "Rhythm" changes in jazz, in the key of B♭. Many jazz tunes have been written on these changes, including Gershwin's "I Got Rhythm."

You'll notice that when you get to the B-section or "release," you can walk the bass line up in a step-wise progression.

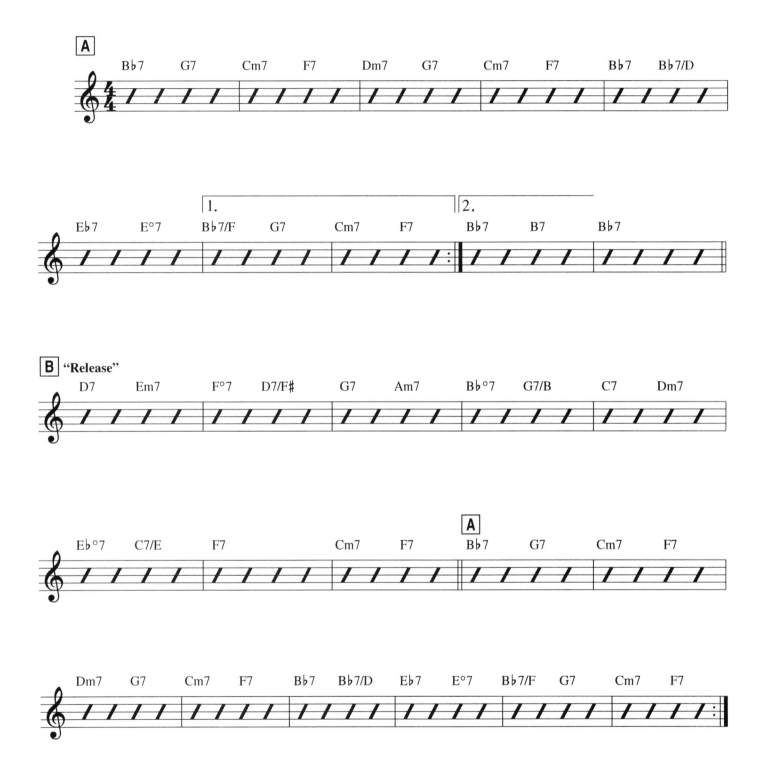

◆28 "Rhythm" Changes Breakdown

This is a form we call A–A–B–A.

A more common release as played by many great bebop artists is as follows:

Optional release for "Rhythm" changes

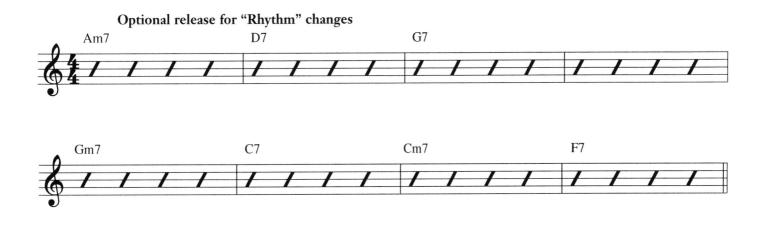

◆29 Scale Tones

Below I've written out the first two bars of "Rhythm" changes, with scale tones for each chord to use in your melodic improvisation.

Scale tones on "Rhythm" changes (first two bars)

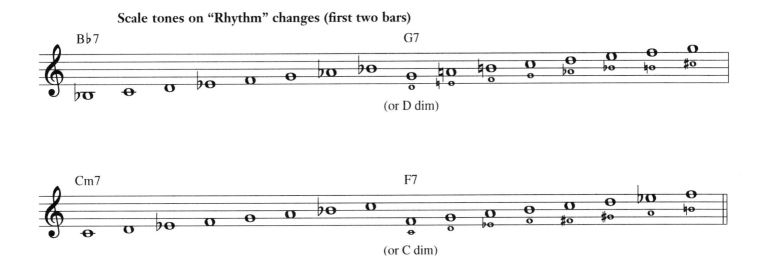

◆30 Diminished Scales

It's time to introduce another kind of scale, the diminished scale.

The diminished scale is playing a whole step, then a half-step, then a whole step, then a half step, and so on.

Therefore, starting on D, the D diminished scale is as follows:

D Diminished Scale

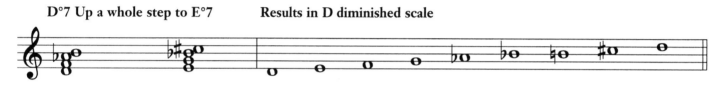

You'll notice that the notes of the scale make up two superimposed seventh chords, built one step apart.

D°7 Up a whole step to E°7   **Results in D diminished scale**

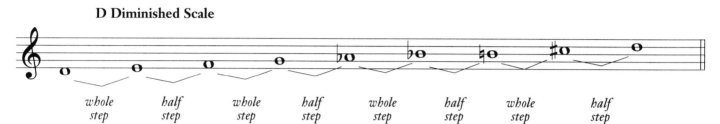

The diminished scale is a nice choice for a seventh chord with a flatted ninth. The following example could be applied to the third and fourth bars of the "Rhythm" changes we used previously.

Using flat ninth chords and corresponding diminished scales

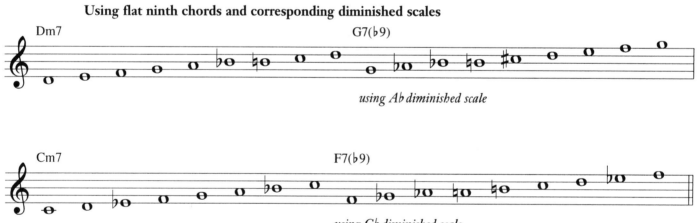

Use of these scales opens up some horizons as to what notes will fit well in our improvisation.

◆31 "Rhythm" Changes Breakdown Continued

Let's look at the last four bars of the "Rhythm" changes, beginning with B♭7, to B♭/D to E♭7 to E°7 (or E diminished seventh).

The diminished chord is something new, since we haven't dealt with diminished chords up to this point. The diminished seventh chord is made up of stacked minor thirds.

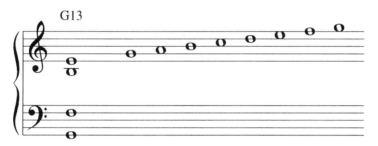

Next is B♭/F and then G13. Note that G13, spelled G–F–B–E, doesn't change our scale tones, which are still the tones of a G7 chord.

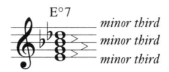

The last example illustrates common scales and chords used in the last four bars of "Rhythm" changes. It should be noted that the G diminished scale is not the diminished scale to use over a G7 chord. Use the A♭ diminished scale for the G7, the E♭ diminished over the D7 chord, and so on.

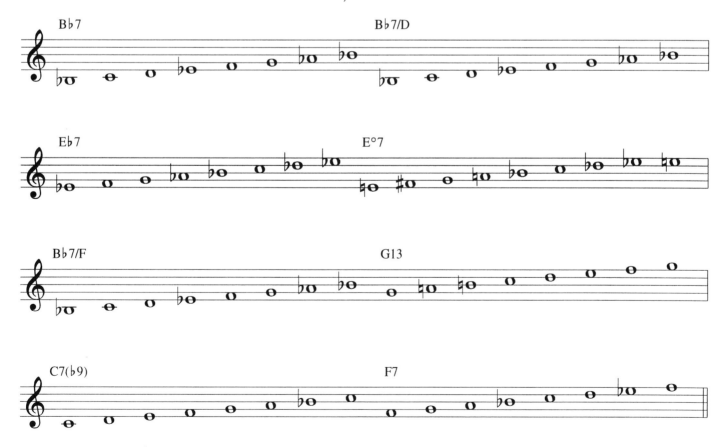

◆ Putting It Together

Listen to the recording to hear what the whole thing put together sounds like.

◆ End Talk

I've been playing jazz for years and here I am trying to condense my knowledge into short form.

Remember that becoming a good jazz pianist is not going to happen overnight. It takes years and years to become a good jazz improviser. You have to take the music apart and work slowly. Don't get discouraged. It takes time. And don't be afraid to ask more experienced players for knowledge or advice.

I've been happy to help guide you. Remember that this is just one viewpoint out of the billions of viewpoints on our planet.

Listening to recordings is very important. Find the things that you like and study them closely.

Don't play too much. Don't burn yourself out mentally or physically. As a pianist, you can hurt yourself if you play too much. Pace yourself.

Always listen to what you're playing. Be patient with yourself.

Take frequent breaks. I like to work intensely for ten minutes or so and then take a short break so I can be fresh when I come back.

Don't get bored or discouraged. There's so much beauty and love in the jazz piano literature that there's no reason to ever get bored.

Finally, I wish you luck and I hope to hear you play someday.

◆ End Music

Continue Your Studies With
Warren Bernhardt!

If you enjoyed this Listen & Learn Publication, you'll want to know about other terrific piano instruction products by Warren Bernhardt.

VIDEO LESSONS

You Can Play Jazz Piano - Three 90-minute videos.

Video One: Getting Started (VD-BER-JP01)
Learn basic hand positions and scales; diatonic thirds and triads; chord inversions and voicings; melodic improvisation and ornamentation; the 2-5-1 chord progression and its variations; tri-tones and scales for playing blues; and much more.

Video Two: Basic Keyboard Harmony (VD-BER-JP02)
Covers chords and intervals, progressions, substitutions and inversions, voice leading, bass lines and melodic accompaniment. Includes improvisational techniques and special exercises for furthering musical understanding and ability.

Video Three: Soloing And Performing (VD-BER-JP03)
Topics include scales for soloing and improvisation; "setting up" a solo; preparing a song for performance; playing with other musicians and more. Four original jazz etudes provide wonderful practice sessions: *Sara's Touch*, *Pali Lookout*, *Ain't Life Grand?* and *B-Loose Blues.*

AUDIO CASSETTE LESSONS

Warren Bernhardt Teaches Jazz Piano (AD-BER-JP) - Six one-hour audio cassettes and music book.
This series was digitally remastered and edited to create Warren Bernhardt's *Listen & Learn* publications. If you'd like more detailed instruction on the topics included on this book/CD - plus lots more - you'll want to purchase this complete six-hour cassette series.

*These and hundreds of other top instructional tapes are available
from your music dealer or directly from Homespun Tapes.
For complete catalog, write or call:*

Box 694 • Woodstock, NY 12498 • (800) 33-TAPES